Title: Unleashing Your Inner Power: Mastering Motivation, Mind Control, and Positive Thinking

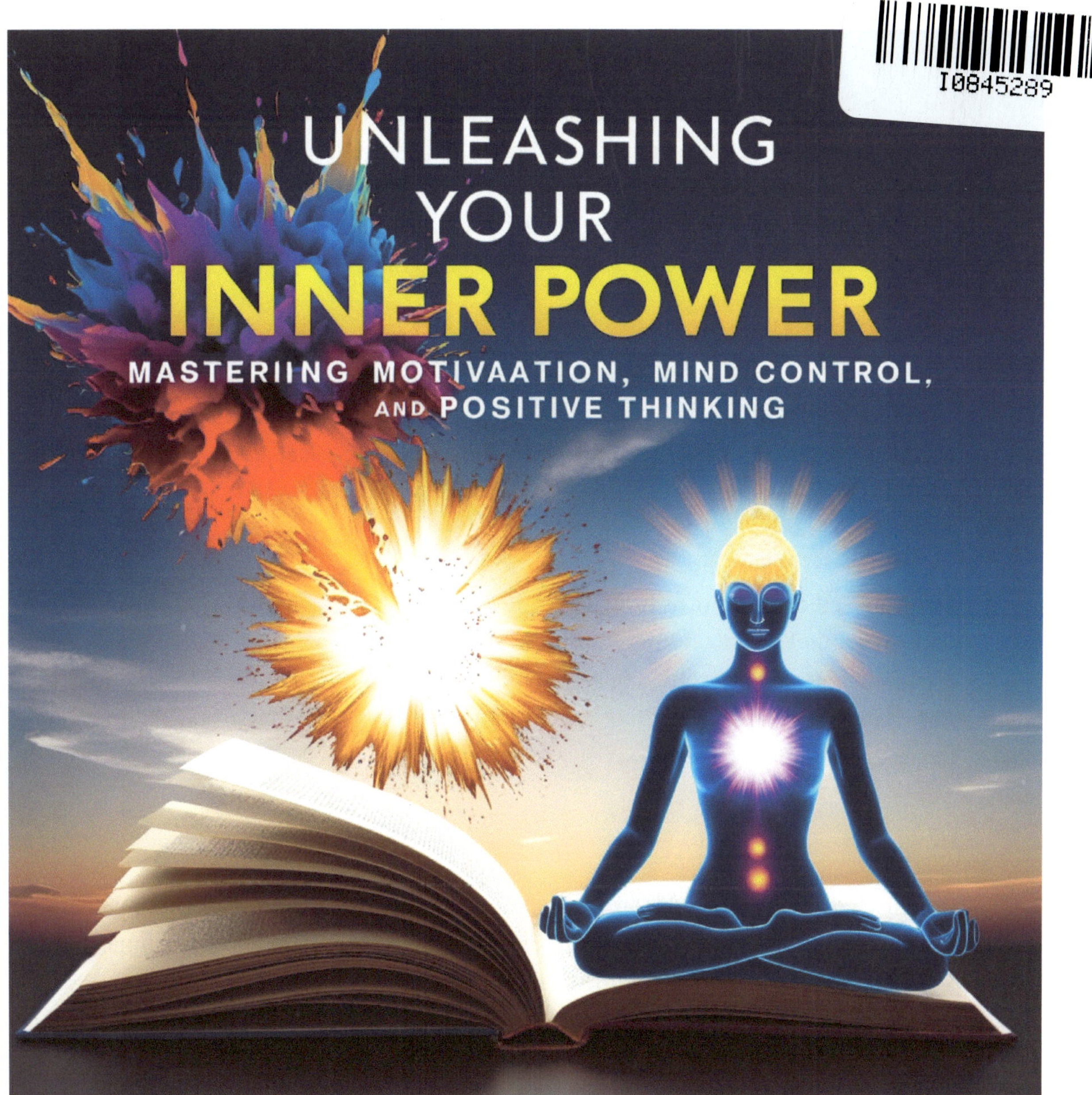

Introduction: Awakening the Power Within

In this fast-paced world, the greatest untapped resource lies within our minds. Whether you aim to lead, grow, or transform, the journey starts with the mastery of your mental faculties. This book will guide you through the art of motivation, mind control, positive thinking, and the deep powers locked within your subconscious. As you turn each page, you will gain practical techniques to unleash your true potential and become a master of your own destiny

Chapter 1: The Science of Motivation

1.1 The Biological Basis of Motivation

Motivation is more than just a mental concept; it has a biological foundation rooted in the brain's chemistry. Neuroscience shows that motivation is closely linked to the brain's reward system, primarily governed by the neurotransmitter dopamine. When we set a goal or engage in a new task, dopamine is released, and it fuels our desire to achieve that goal. This is why we feel a surge of energy when we're about to start something exciting.

- **The Role of Dopamine:** Dopamine doesn't just make us feel pleasure; it also propels us to take action. It acts as a "motivator" that pushes us toward a reward. When we visualize the success of achieving a goal, dopamine is released even before we've reached the finish line, stimulating our brain to work harder.

- **The Reward System in Action:** Imagine you're starting a fitness journey. The first time you complete a workout, your brain releases dopamine, giving you a sense of accomplishment. Each time you return to the gym, your brain anticipates the reward (the dopamine release) and motivates you to keep going. This creates a positive feedback loop.

Understanding this connection helps us recognize that motivation is not something that comes and goes randomly; it's part of our brain's design. Learning to trigger these dopamine surges can help you sustain motivation over time.

1.2 Intrinsic vs. Extrinsic Motivation

There are two primary types of motivation: intrinsic and extrinsic. Both play a role in driving us toward our goals, but they work in very different ways.

- **Intrinsic Motivation:** This is the motivation that comes from within. It's driven by personal satisfaction, passion, and a deep sense of purpose. When you're intrinsically motivated, you're not focused on external rewards but on the joy or fulfillment the activity brings. For example, someone who paints because they love expressing themselves through art is intrinsically motivated.

- **Benefits of Intrinsic Motivation:** Long-lasting and self-sustaining. Since the motivation comes from within, it doesn't rely on external factors that might change or disappear. This form of motivation leads to greater creativity, fulfillment, and overall well-being. People who are intrinsically motivated often perform better in the long run because they are genuinely invested in the process, not just the outcome.

- **Cultivating Intrinsic Motivation:** One way to develop intrinsic motivation is by aligning your goals with your values and passions. Ask yourself, "Why is this important to me? What personal meaning does this goal hold?" This deepens your connection to the task at hand and makes the journey more enjoyable, rather than a burden.

- **Extrinsic Motivation:** This type of motivation is driven by external rewards or pressures, such as money, recognition, or avoiding punishment. For example, someone may work overtime because they want to earn a bonus or impress their boss.

- **Benefits of Extrinsic Motivation:** Extrinsic motivation is effective for short-term goals, like meeting deadlines or achieving quick wins. It's also useful in situations where tasks might not be inherently enjoyable but necessary (e.g., studying for an exam).

- **Limitations of Extrinsic Motivation:** While extrinsic motivation can be powerful, it's not always sustainable. Once the external reward is removed or achieved, motivation may fade. Relying solely on extrinsic motivation can lead to burnout or a lack of fulfillment over time.

Balancing Both Types of Motivation: Ideally, you want to balance intrinsic and extrinsic motivators. For example, if you're working on a project, you can focus on both the personal satisfaction of completing it (intrinsic) and the recognition or rewards you'll receive (extrinsic). This creates a more robust motivational framework.

1.3 Harnessing Your "Why": The Core of Motivation

Understanding your "why" is essential for lasting motivation. Your "why" is the deeper reason behind your goals—the emotional or psychological driver that fuels your actions. It answers the question, "Why do I want to achieve this?"

- Finding Your "Why": To discover your true motivation, take some time to reflect on your goals. Ask yourself:

- Why does this goal matter to me?

- How will achieving this improve my life or the lives of others?

- What personal values does this goal align with?

- What would happen if I didn't achieve this goal?

When you're clear on your "why," it becomes easier to stay motivated, even when challenges arise. For example, if your goal is to build a successful business, your "why" might be financial freedom, creating a legacy, or helping others. This deeper motivation will keep you going when times get tough.

Exercise: Discovering Your "Why"

Take a piece of paper and write down your top 3 goals. For each goal, answer the following:

1. What will achieving this goal bring me?

2. How will it change my life?

3. What will happen if I don't achieve it?

This process helps clarify the emotional drivers behind your goals, which strengthens your motivation.

1.4 Building Momentum: The Snowball Effect

Motivation thrives on momentum. The more you achieve, the more motivated you feel to continue achieving. This is known as the **snowball effect**—small actions lead to bigger results over time, eventually creating a powerful cycle of growth and achievement.

- **Starting Small:** One of the biggest mistakes people make is setting overly ambitious goals right from the start. This can lead to frustration and loss of motivation. Instead, focus on small, achievable goals that build momentum. For example, if your ultimate goal is to run a marathon, start by running a mile each day. As you gain confidence and endurance, you can gradually increase the distance.

- **Why Small Wins Matter:** Small wins boost confidence and generate the dopamine that fuels motivation. Each time you achieve a mini-goal, your brain registers it as a success, which reinforces the belief that you can achieve more.

- **The Power of Habit:** Habits play a crucial role in building momentum. By turning small tasks into daily habits, you remove the need for constant motivation. Habits, once formed, become automatic, making it easier to stay on track.

- **Creating Powerful Habits:** Start with one or two small, specific actions that contribute to your larger goal. For example, if you want to write a book, commit to writing 200 words every day. Over time, this small habit can accumulate into significant progress.

1.5 Overcoming Procrastination: Motivation's Greatest Enemy

Procrastination is one of the biggest obstacles to motivation. It's the act of delaying tasks, often because we fear failure, feel overwhelmed, or lack clarity on where to start.

- **The Psychology Behind Procrastination:** Procrastination is often driven by fear or avoidance. When a task feels too big or uncertain, the brain seeks out distractions to avoid discomfort. This leads to a temporary sense of relief, but over time, it creates stress and guilt, which further lowers motivation.

- **Breaking the Cycle:** The key to overcoming procrastination is to reduce the perceived difficulty of the task. One way to do this is by breaking the task down into smaller, more manageable steps. This lowers the mental barrier to getting started and makes the task seem less overwhelming.

- **The Two-Minute Rule:** A simple technique for overcoming procrastination is the "Two-Minute Rule." The idea is to commit to working on a task for just two minutes. Often, the hardest part is getting started, and once you've begun, you're likely to keep going. By setting a small, non-intimidating time limit, you trick your brain into taking action.

Chapter 2: Mind Control: Training the Inner Self

2.1 Controlling Your Thoughts: The Power of Focus

Your mind is a battleground where thousands of thoughts pass daily. To control your mind, the first step is to understand that not all thoughts are valuable. Some are distractions, while others serve as guidance toward your goals. Learning to focus only on the thoughts that serve your purpose is the key to mastering your mind.

- **Selective Focus:** In our modern world, distractions are everywhere, from social media to daily stressors. Selective focus is the skill of filtering out unnecessary thoughts and concentrating on what truly matters. The mind works best when focused on one task at a time, so by training yourself to focus deeply, you enhance productivity and clarity.

- **Technique: The Pomodoro Method:** One of the most effective ways to train focus is the Pomodoro Technique. Set a timer for 25 minutes, during which you focus exclusively on a task, followed by a 5-minute break. This creates short bursts of intense concentration, which improves focus over time. Use this technique to train your mind to concentrate for longer periods without distractions.

2.2 The Power of Mental Discipline

Mental discipline is about controlling impulsive reactions, emotional fluctuations, and the urge to quit when faced with challenges. Like a muscle, mental discipline grows stronger with consistent practice. This ability enables you to persist through obstacles, maintain emotional stability, and stay committed to your goals.

- **Mindfulness and Meditation:** Practicing mindfulness and meditation is an excellent way to enhance mental discipline. Mindfulness involves staying fully present in the moment, observing your thoughts without judgment. It teaches you to manage emotions, reduce stress, and keep your mind grounded.

- **Exercise: The 5-Minute Meditation:** Start by setting aside just five minutes each day for meditation. Sit quietly, close your eyes, and focus on your breathing. If thoughts wander, gently bring your attention back to your breath. Over time, this practice will help you become more aware of your mental patterns and improve your ability to control your thoughts.

- **Building Mental Toughness:** Mental toughness is the ability to push through discomfort and adversity. To develop it, challenge yourself regularly by stepping outside your comfort zone. Whether it's through physical challenges, learning new skills, or pushing through difficult work, each experience builds resilience and strengthens your ability to stay focused under pressure.

2.3 Breaking Free from Limiting Beliefs

Limiting beliefs are mental barriers that hold you back from reaching your full potential. These beliefs often stem from childhood, past failures, or societal conditioning. They manifest as thoughts like, "I'm not good enough," "I'll never succeed," or "I'm too old to learn." These beliefs operate on a subconscious level and sabotage your progress.

- **Identifying Limiting Beliefs:** The first step to breaking free is to identify the limiting beliefs you hold. Pay attention to the recurring negative thoughts that arise when you're trying something new or facing a challenge. Write them down and analyze where they might have originated.

- **Exercise: Reframing Limiting Beliefs:** Once you've identified a limiting belief, the next step is to reframe it. For example, if you constantly think, "I'm not smart enough to succeed," replace it with, "I'm capable of learning anything with effort and persistence." By consciously replacing negative beliefs with empowering ones, you begin to rewire your brain for success.

2.4 The Art of Mental Rehearsal

Mental rehearsal, also known as visualization, is a powerful technique used by athletes, performers, and successful individuals to achieve their goals. It involves mentally practicing an event or action before it occurs, programming the mind for success.

- **How Mental Rehearsal Works:** When you vividly imagine yourself performing a task, your brain activates the same neural pathways as it would if you were physically doing it. This primes your mind for success and reduces anxiety or fear associated with the task.

- **Exercise: Visualizing Success:** Close your eyes and visualize yourself achieving a specific goal. Imagine every detail—how it feels, what the environment looks like, and the emotions you experience upon success. Repeat this visualization daily, and your brain will become accustomed to the idea of success, making it easier to achieve in real life.

2.5 Strengthening the Mind-Body Connection

The mind and body are deeply connected, and each affects the other. When you train your mind, you also train your body to perform at higher levels. Similarly, maintaining physical health improves mental clarity, focus, and resilience.

- **Exercise and the Mind:** Physical exercise is one of the best ways to improve mental control. Exercise releases endorphins, which enhance mood and reduce stress. Regular movement also increases blood flow to the brain, sharpening mental focus and memory.

- **Incorporating Mindful Movement:** Practices like yoga, tai chi, or mindful walking can enhance both physical and mental control. These activities require you to synchronize breath with movement, promoting greater awareness of the mind-body connection and cultivating mental calmness.

Chapter 3: The Power of Positive Thinking

3.1 What is Positive Thinking?

Positive thinking is not about ignoring life's challenges or pretending everything is perfect. Instead, it's about approaching life with a constructive and optimistic mindset. It's the ability to focus on solutions rather than problems and see opportunities in every situation.

- **The Realism of Positivity:** Positive thinking doesn't mean ignoring reality or being blindly optimistic. It's about acknowledging challenges while maintaining a belief in your ability to overcome them. It's rooted in the understanding that while you can't control everything, you can always control how you respond to situations.

- **Reframing Challenges:** Positive thinkers often reframe difficult situations into opportunities for growth. For example, instead of thinking, "This project is too difficult," you can reframe it as, "This is an opportunity to learn new skills and overcome a challenge." This shift in perspective can dramatically improve your outlook and performance.

3.2 Emotional Benefits of Positive Thinking

Positive thinking has profound effects on mental and emotional well-being. Studies show that people with a positive outlook experience lower levels of stress, higher emotional resilience, and better overall mental health.

- **Reduced Stress Levels:** Positive thinkers are better equipped to manage stress because they tend to focus on solutions rather than dwelling on problems. This proactive approach reduces anxiety and prevents situations from becoming overwhelming.

- **Exercise: Gratitude Practice:** One way to cultivate positive thinking is through a daily gratitude practice. Each day, write down three things you're grateful for. This simple exercise shifts your focus from what's lacking to what's abundant, rewiring your brain to notice the positive aspects of life.

- **Emotional Resilience:** Positive thinking builds emotional resilience, allowing you to bounce back quickly from setbacks. When faced with failure, positive thinkers view it as a learning experience rather than a personal shortcoming, which helps them recover faster and stay motivated.

3.3 The Law of Attraction

The Law of Attraction is the belief that positive or negative thoughts bring positive or negative experiences into a person's life. According to this principle, like attracts like. By focusing on positive thoughts, you attract positive outcomes, while dwelling on negative thoughts draws negative experiences.

- **How the Law of Attraction Works:** When you consistently think positively about your goals and dreams, you train your mind to seek out opportunities and solutions that align with those thoughts. This doesn't mean magical thinking, but rather, your mindset influences your actions, and your actions influence your results.

- **Visualization and Affirmations:** Visualization and affirmations are key tools in the Law of Attraction. Visualizing your goals as if they've already been achieved helps align your thoughts with your desired outcome. Similarly, repeating positive affirmations daily trains your subconscious to believe in the possibility of success.

3.4 Affirmations and the Power of Words

Words have power. The words you speak to yourself, whether out loud or internally, shape your thoughts, emotions, and actions. Positive affirmations are statements you repeat to yourself to reinforce a positive self-image and mindset.

- **Creating Effective Affirmations:** The key to effective affirmations is to make them specific, positive, and present-tense. For example, instead of saying, "I will be successful," say, "I am successful." This reaffirms your belief in your ability to achieve your goals in the present moment.

- **Exercise: Daily Affirmation Practice:** Start your day by standing in front of a mirror and repeating a few positive affirmations. Statements like, "I am capable," "I attract success," or "I am confident in my abilities" can boost your self-esteem and set a positive tone for the day.

3.5 Building a Positive Environment

Your environment plays a significant role in your ability to maintain a positive mindset. Surrounding yourself with positive influences—whether through people, spaces, or media—creates a foundation for positivity to thrive.

- **The People You Surround Yourself With:** Positive people uplift and inspire you, while negative people drain your energy and reinforce limiting beliefs. Make a conscious effort to spend time with those who encourage growth, positivity, and optimism.

- **Creating a Supportive Space:** Your physical environment also influences your mindset. Decluttering your space, adding elements that inspire joy (like plants, art, or meaningful objects), and removing distractions create an environment that fosters clarity and positivity.

Chapter 4: The Leader in Yourself

4.1 Understanding Leadership: It Starts from Within

Leadership isn't just about managing others; it's about leading yourself first. True leadership begins with self-mastery—the ability to take charge of your emotions, thoughts, and actions. Before you can lead a team or influence others, you must develop a deep understanding of your own values, strengths, and vision.

- **Self-Awareness as the Foundation of Leadership:** Self-awareness is the cornerstone of effective leadership. It involves being aware of your emotions, motivations, and how you are perceived by others. Leaders who possess self-awareness are better equipped to make decisions aligned with their core values, manage their weaknesses, and leverage their strengths.

- **Exercise: Reflecting on Your Strengths and Weaknesses:** Take time to evaluate your personal strengths and weaknesses. What qualities make you a strong leader, and what areas need improvement? Being honest with yourself helps you become a more authentic and effective leader.

- **Developing Emotional Intelligence (EQ):** Emotional intelligence is the ability to recognize and manage your emotions while understanding the emotions of others. High EQ is critical for leadership because it enables you to connect with your team, handle conflict effectively, and inspire trust.

- **Components of Emotional Intelligence:**

  - **Self-regulation:** Controlling impulsive behaviors and maintaining composure in challenging situations.

  - **Empathy:** Understanding the feelings and perspectives of others.

  - **Social Skills:** Building strong relationships and communicating effectively.

- **Practice EQ in Daily Life:** Start by observing your emotional responses in various situations. When you encounter conflict or stress, pause before reacting, and think about how your response will impact those around you.

4.2 Vision: Crafting a Compelling Future

Great leaders possess a clear and compelling vision. They see beyond the present and chart a course toward a better future. Your vision is the driving force that guides your decisions and actions. It motivates not only yourself but also those around you, providing a sense of direction and purpose.

- **Creating Your Personal Vision:** What kind of leader do you want to be? What impact do you want to have on your life, your family, your community, or the world? A personal vision isn't just about professional achievements; it encompasses the life you want to lead, the values you want to uphold, and the legacy you wish to leave behind.

- **Exercise: Defining Your Leadership Vision:** Write down your leadership vision. Think about where you want to be in 5 or 10 years, and consider the personal qualities you'll need to develop to get there. This exercise provides clarity and helps align your daily actions with long-term goals.

- **Communicating Your Vision:** Once you have a clear vision, the next step is to communicate it effectively. Whether you're leading a team or inspiring others, your ability to articulate your vision with passion and clarity will inspire those around you to follow your lead.

4.3 Taking Initiative: The Hallmark of a Leader

Leaders don't wait for opportunities—they create them. Taking initiative means stepping up, even when it's uncomfortable or outside of your designated role. It's about being proactive, solving problems, and pushing boundaries to achieve results.

- **Cultivating a Bias for Action:** One trait that distinguishes successful leaders is their ability to act decisively, even in the face of uncertainty. Taking initiative often means stepping into unknown territory, but it's also where the greatest opportunities for growth and success lie.

- **Exercise: Acting Outside Your Comfort Zone:** Identify one area in your life or career where you've been hesitant to take action. Commit to stepping up and taking initiative, whether it's volunteering for a challenging project, starting a new venture, or having a difficult conversation.

4.4 Inspiring and Leading Others

True leadership is not about control or authority; it's about inspiring others to achieve their best. Great leaders create environments that empower and uplift their teams, encouraging collaboration, creativity, and ownership.

- **Building Trust and Respect:** Trust is the foundation of all great leadership. To inspire others, you must earn their trust by being consistent, transparent, and accountable. Respect is also crucial—people follow leaders who respect their time, opinions, and talents.

- **Exercise: Practicing Active Listening:** One way to build trust and respect is through active listening. When interacting with others, focus on truly understanding their perspectives, without interrupting or preparing your response. This shows that you value their input and fosters stronger relationships.

- **Empowering Your Team:** Leaders succeed when their teams succeed. Empower those around you by providing clear expectations, offering support, and allowing them the autonomy to make decisions. Empowerment boosts confidence and engagement, resulting in better overall performance.

4.5 Resilience: Leading Through Adversity

Leadership is not without challenges. Resilience is the ability to lead through adversity, bounce back from setbacks, and remain committed to your vision despite difficulties.

- **Developing Resilience:** Resilience comes from maintaining a positive outlook and finding opportunities in challenges. When setbacks occur, resilient leaders ask, "What can I learn from this?" rather than focusing on the failure itself.

- **Exercise: Building a Resilience Plan:** Reflect on past challenges in your life. What strategies helped you overcome them? How can you apply these lessons to future obstacles? Having a resilience plan prepares you for tough times and helps you navigate them with confidence.

Chapter 5: The Powers of the Subconscious Mind

5.1 Understanding the Subconscious Mind

Your subconscious mind is like a vast, untapped reservoir of power. It controls much of your behavior, habits, and emotional responses without you being consciously aware of it. While the conscious mind handles day-to-day decision-making, the subconscious is constantly at work in the background, processing information, and influencing your thoughts and actions.

- **How the Subconscious Mind Works:** The subconscious is responsible for habits, beliefs, and automatic responses. When you repeatedly think or do something, it gets stored in the subconscious, eventually becoming part of your identity. For example, if you frequently think, "I'm not good at public speaking," your subconscious accepts this as truth, reinforcing your fear of public speaking.

- **The Subconscious as a Servant:** The subconscious mind doesn't judge or reason; it simply acts on the information it receives from the conscious mind. This means that by intentionally feeding your subconscious positive and empowering thoughts, you can reprogram it to work in your favor.

5.2 Reprogramming Your Subconscious Mind for Success

One of the most powerful ways to transform your life is by consciously reprogramming your subconscious mind. This requires consistency, but once your subconscious is aligned with your conscious desires, achieving your goals becomes far easier.

- **Positive Affirmations and Self-Talk:** Positive affirmations are statements that reinforce empowering beliefs. Repeating affirmations daily helps override negative thoughts stored in the subconscious. Over time, your subconscious will accept these affirmations as truth, influencing your thoughts and actions in a positive direction.

- **Exercise: Creating Personal Affirmations:** Write down 5-10 positive affirmations related to your goals. For example, if you want to become more confident, affirm, "I am confident and capable in every situation." Repeat these affirmations each morning and before bed, allowing them to sink into your subconscious.

- **Visualization and Mental Rehearsal:** Visualization is another powerful tool for reprogramming the subconscious. By vividly imagining yourself achieving a goal, you create a mental blueprint for success. The subconscious mind cannot differentiate between real and imagined experiences, so it treats your visualization as if it were happening in reality.

- **Exercise: Visualizing Success:** Set aside time each day to visualize your goals. Picture yourself in vivid detail living the life you desire—whether it's achieving career success, improving relationships, or mastering a new skill. Engage all your senses in the visualization to make it as realistic as possible.

5.3 The Power of Belief

Your subconscious is heavily influenced by your core beliefs—both positive and negative. Beliefs are the mental filters through which you interpret the world. They shape your reality because you tend to act in accordance with what you believe to be true.

- **Identifying Limiting Beliefs:** Limiting beliefs are deeply ingrained and often go unnoticed, but they can sabotage your success. Common limiting beliefs include, "I'm not smart enough," "I don't deserve success," or "Money is hard to come by."

- **Exercise: Challenging Limiting Beliefs:** To identify limiting beliefs, reflect on areas of your life where you feel stuck or unsatisfied. Ask yourself, "What belief is holding me back in this area?" Once identified, challenge the belief by asking, "Is this belief absolutely true?" and replace it with a more empowering belief.

5.4 Habits: Programming the Subconscious for Success

Habits are automatic behaviors controlled by the subconscious mind. Developing positive habits is one of the most effective ways to harness the power of your subconscious for long-term success.

- **Building Positive Habits:** The key to habit formation is repetition and consistency. Start with small, manageable habits that align with your goals. Over time, these habits become automatic, making it easier to stay on track without relying on conscious effort.

- **Exercise: Habit Stacking:** One technique for building new habits is "habit stacking," where you attach a new habit to an existing one. For example, if you want to start meditating daily, you can stack this habit onto your morning

Coffee routine. By linking the new habit to something you already do, it becomes easier to establish.

5.5 Unlocking Creative Potential

Your subconscious mind is also the source of your creativity and intuition. When you relax your conscious mind, the subconscious can provide solutions and ideas that you might not have considered otherwise.

- **Accessing Subconscious Creativity:** Many people experience flashes of creativity during activities like walking, showering, or drifting off to sleep. These moments occur because the conscious mind is at rest, allowing the subconscious to come forward with insights.

- **Exercise: Freewriting for Creativity:** One way to tap into your subconscious creativity is through freewriting. Set a timer for 10 minutes and write continuously without filtering or editing your thoughts. This stream-of-consciousness exercise bypasses the conscious mind's critical filter, allowing the subconscious to express itself freely.

Chapter 6: Harnessing the Power of Your Mind for Daily Success

6.1 The Importance of Mental Clarity

In today's fast-paced world, mental clarity is one of the most valuable assets you can cultivate. A clear mind helps you focus, make better decisions, and navigate daily tasks with ease. Cluttered thoughts and overwhelming distractions, on the other hand, reduce productivity and cause stress.

- **Achieving Mental Clarity:** Mental clarity comes from organizing your thoughts and staying present in the moment. When your mind is scattered, it's harder to be productive or efficient. By clearing mental clutter and focusing on what truly matters, you can approach each task with a sharper, more focused mindset.

- **Exercise: Daily Brain Dump:** Set aside time at the beginning of each day to perform a "brain dump." Write down everything on your mind—whether it's work-related, personal, or general thoughts. By putting these thoughts on paper, you clear mental space and free your mind for focused work.

6.2 Setting Daily Intentions

Setting clear intentions at the start of your day gives your mind a sense of direction. When you set an intention, you're telling your mind what to focus on, which helps prioritize tasks and maintain alignment with your goals.

- **The Power of Intention Setting:** Instead of simply going through the motions of your day, setting an intention gives you purpose. This practice helps you focus on specific goals, behaviors, or attitudes you want to embody.

- **Exercise: Morning Intentions Practice:** Each morning, take a few minutes to sit in stillness and set a positive intention for the day. For example, you might decide, "Today, I will focus on being patient and productive." Repeat this intention to yourself, and let it guide your actions throughout the day.

6.3 The Role of Visualization in Daily Success

Visualization isn't just for long-term goals; it's also a powerful tool to guide your daily actions. By visualizing success at the start of the day, you prepare your mind for the outcomes you want to achieve.

- **Visualizing Your Day:** Before starting your tasks, take a moment to mentally rehearse how you want your day to unfold. Imagine completing your most important tasks, interacting positively with others, and overcoming any challenges that might arise. This practice sets your mind up for success, aligning your actions with the outcomes you desire.

- **Exercise: Visualize Your Daily Wins:** Spend 5 minutes in the morning visualizing specific moments of success during your day. Whether it's nailing a presentation, finishing a project, or handling a tough conversation with ease, focus on the positive results you want to create.

6.4 Using Affirmations to Boost Confidence

Affirmations help you align your subconscious mind with positive self-perception, which in turn enhances confidence and reduces self-doubt. Incorporating affirmations into your daily routine can boost your belief in your abilities and help you tackle challenges with a positive attitude.

- **Daily Affirmation Practice:** Choose affirmations that resonate with your goals and repeat them throughout the day. For example, affirmations like "I am focused and capable" or "I approach every challenge with confidence" can reinforce a positive mindset.

- **Exercise: Personalized Affirmation Cards:** Write down 3-5 affirmations on small index cards and place them where you'll see them throughout the day—on your desk, mirror, or phone screen. Each time you see the cards, repeat the affirmations to yourself, reaffirming your confidence and ability.

6.5 Managing Your Energy, Not Just Your Time

Success is not just about managing time—it's about managing energy. Your mental and physical energy levels fluctuate throughout the day, and knowing when you're at your best can help you optimize productivity.

- **Understanding Your Energy Cycles:** Pay attention to when you feel most focused and alert during the day. Some people are most productive in the morning, while others hit their stride in the afternoon. Align your most important tasks with your peak energy levels to maximize effectiveness.

- **Exercise: Tracking Energy Levels:** Over the next few days, note how your energy fluctuates. When do you feel most focused? When do you experience fatigue? Use this information to adjust your schedule, tackling challenging tasks when your energy is high and saving lighter tasks for when it dips.

6.6 The Power of Gratitude for Daily Success

Gratitude is a simple but powerful practice that shifts your mindset from scarcity to abundance. When you focus on what you're grateful for, you train your mind to see the positives in every situation, which boosts resilience, happiness, and success.

- **Gratitude as a Mental Habit:** Incorporating gratitude into your daily routine helps you stay focused on the good things happening in your life, even amid challenges. This positive focus boosts mental well-being and encourages success-oriented behavior.

- **Exercise: Daily Gratitude Journal:** At the end of each day, write down three things you're grateful for. They can be small wins, kind interactions, or lessons learned. This practice rewires your brain to notice and appreciate the positive aspects of life, setting you up for long-term success.

Chapter 7: Overcoming Obstacles with Mind Mastery

7.1 Reframing Obstacles as Opportunities

Obstacles are an inevitable part of life, but the way you perceive them makes all the difference. With mind mastery, you can reframe obstacles as opportunities for growth and learning, rather than as setbacks or failures.

- **The Power of Perception:** When faced with a challenge, your initial reaction might be frustration or fear. However, by shifting your mindset to view obstacles as temporary and solvable, you empower yourself to find creative solutions.

- **Exercise: Reframing Challenges:** The next time you encounter a challenge, ask yourself, "What can I learn from this situation?" and "How can this make me stronger?" By focusing on growth, you transform challenges into stepping stones toward success.

7.2 Mental Toughness: Persevering in the Face of Adversity

Mental toughness is the ability to stay focused and resilient in the face of adversity. It's about pushing forward, even when the odds seem stacked against you. Building mental toughness helps you navigate life's difficulties with confidence and determination.

- **How to Build Mental Toughness:** Developing mental toughness involves cultivating a "never-give-up" attitude and staying committed to your goals, no matter the challenges. It requires emotional control, perseverance, and the ability to bounce back from failure.

- **Exercise: The Power of Micro-Wins:** Start by tackling small challenges in your life. Each time you overcome a minor obstacle, you build confidence and resilience. These micro-wins add up over time, strengthening your ability to handle larger challenges in the future.

7.3 Letting Go of Fear and Self-Doubt

Fear and self-doubt are two of the most common mental obstacles that hold people back. They often stem from limiting beliefs and past experiences, but with mind mastery, you can overcome these internal barriers.

- **Overcoming Fear:** Fear often arises when you're stepping into the unknown or facing something outside your comfort zone. The key to overcoming fear is to recognize that it's a natural response but not a valid reason to hold yourself back.

- **Exercise: Fear-Setting:** Write down the fears that are holding you back and ask yourself, "What's the worst that could happen?" and "What's the best possible outcome?" Often, the worst-case scenario is less dire than we imagine, and focusing on the best outcome can motivate you to take action.

- **Silencing Self-Doubt:** Self-doubt is a byproduct of negative thinking and insecurity. To silence self-doubt, focus on your past successes and the skills you've developed over time. Every success, no matter how small, is proof of your capability.

- **Exercise: Celebrating Successes:** Create a "success log" where you write down all your achievements, both big and small. When self-doubt creeps in, revisit this log to remind yourself of what you're capable of. This reinforces positive self-belief and boosts confidence.

7.4 The Role of Patience in Overcoming Obstacles

Patience is a key component of mind mastery. Often, success doesn't happen overnight, and obstacles may take time to overcome. Cultivating patience allows you to persist without becoming discouraged or giving up prematurely.

- **Practicing Patience:** When faced with a long-term goal or obstacle, remind yourself that progress takes time. Each small step brings you closer to your desired outcome, even if it doesn't feel like it in the moment.

- **Exercise: The Patience Mindset:** Whenever you feel impatient or frustrated with slow progress, take a moment to reflect on the progress you've already made. Break down your goal into smaller milestones, and celebrate each one as you achieve it. This helps maintain motivation and reinforces the value of persistence.

7.5 The Importance of Flexibility and Adaptability

Life is unpredictable, and obstacles can arise unexpectedly. Mental flexibility—the ability to adapt to changing circumstances—is essential for overcoming challenges. When you're adaptable, you're open to new solutions and aren't rigidly attached to a single plan.

- **Developing Mental Flexibility:** Being mentally flexible doesn't mean abandoning your goals, but rather, adjusting your approach when needed. By staying open to new ideas and strategies, you increase your chances of overcoming obstacles more efficiently.

- **Exercise: Embracing Change:** When something doesn't go as planned, instead of resisting, ask yourself, "What's another way I can achieve my goal?" This shift in perspective opens you up to new possibilities and helps you find creative solutions.

7.6 Mastering the Art of Focus in Challenging Times

When obstacles arise, it's easy to become distracted or lose focus. However, mind mastery involves staying focused on your goals, even when external circumstances are difficult. Developing focus helps you stay on track and avoid distractions that could derail your progress.

- **Building Focus Under Pressure:** When you're facing a tough situation, focus on what you can control, rather than what you can't. This allows you to stay grounded and concentrate on actionable steps rather than getting overwhelmed by the problem itself.

- **Exercise: The Power of the One-Thing Rule:** Identify the single most important thing you can do right now to move closer to your goal. By focusing on one task at a time, you reduce overwhelm and maintain clarity, even in the face of obstacles.

Chapter 8: The Science Behind Positive Thinking

8.1 The Neuroscience of Positive Thinking

Positive thinking isn't just a feel-good concept; it has a real, measurable impact on the brain. When you engage in positive thoughts, the brain releases chemicals like dopamine and serotonin, which enhance mood, motivation, and overall well-being. Over time, this practice rewires the brain, making positive thinking a natural state of mind.

- **How Positive Thinking Rewires the Brain:** The brain has an incredible ability to change and adapt, a phenomenon known as **neuroplasticity**. When you repeatedly focus on positive thoughts, you create new neural pathways that reinforce optimistic thinking patterns. These pathways make it easier for your brain to default to positive thoughts, even during challenging situations.

- **Exercise: The Positivity Circuit**: Each time you catch yourself thinking negatively, consciously replace that thought with a positive one. Over time, this practice helps strengthen the brain's positivity circuit, making it easier to maintain an optimistic mindset.

8.2 The Impact of Positive Thinking on Mental and Physical Health

Research has shown that positive thinking has profound effects on both mental and physical health. People who practice positive thinking are less likely to suffer from depression, anxiety, and stress-related illnesses. They also tend to live longer, healthier lives.

- **Mental Health Benefits**: Positive thinking reduces the production of stress hormones like cortisol, which in turn lowers anxiety and improves emotional resilience. Optimistic individuals also experience higher levels of life satisfaction and are more adept at coping with adversity.

- **Physical Health Benefits:** Studies have found that positive thinking boosts the immune system, lowers the risk of cardiovascular disease, and promotes faster recovery from illness or injury. The mind-body connection is powerful, and positive thinking strengthens this bond, leading to better overall health.

- **Exercise: Daily Gratitude Meditation:** Incorporate a 5-10 minute gratitude meditation into your daily routine. Sit quietly, close your eyes, and focus on things you're grateful for—whether it's your health, relationships, or accomplishments. This practice activates positive emotions and contributes to long-term mental and physical well-being.

8.3 The Broaden-and-Build Theory of Positive Emotions

The **Broaden-and-Build Theory** by psychologist Barbara Fredrickson explains how positive emotions expand our awareness and encourage us to think more creatively and openly. When we're in a positive state of mind, we're more likely to see new possibilities, form stronger relationships, and tackle challenges with resilience.

- **Broadening Your Mindset:** Positive emotions like joy, gratitude, and love help you see the bigger picture and open your mind to new ideas. This broadened perspective allows for greater problem-solving abilities and increased creativity.

- **Building Lasting Resources:** Positive thinking doesn't just make you feel good in the moment; it builds lasting psychological resources like resilience, emotional intelligence, and mental agility. Over time, these resources help you navigate life's challenges with greater ease.

- **Exercise: Practicing Positive Emotions:** Make a conscious effort to experience positive emotions throughout the day. Whether it's laughing with a friend, appreciating nature, or enjoying a hobby, these moments of joy and gratitude broaden your perspective and build long-term resilience.

8.4 The Power of Optimism: How Positive Expectations Shape Reality

Optimism is a key component of positive thinking. It's the belief that good things are going to happen, and that you have the ability to overcome obstacles. Research has shown that optimistic individuals tend to achieve higher levels of success because they're more likely to persist in the face of adversity.

- **The Self-Fulfilling Prophecy of Optimism:** Optimism creates a **self-fulfilling prophecy.** When you expect good things to happen, you're more likely to take action that leads to positive outcomes. Conversely, pessimistic expectations can lead to inaction or self-sabotage, which reinforce negative outcomes.

- **Exercise: Shifting to an Optimistic Mindset:** The next time you face a challenge, consciously choose to view it through an optimistic lens. Ask yourself, "What's the best possible outcome in this situation?" and "What can I do to make that outcome a reality?" This shift in perspective helps you stay motivated and proactive.

8.5 Positive Thinking and the Law of Attraction

The **Law of Attraction** suggests that like attracts like—positive thoughts attract positive experiences, and negative thoughts attract negative outcomes. By focusing on what you want (rather than what you don't want), you align your energy with your desires, making it easier to manifest them in.

Conclusion: Becoming the Master of Your Mind

The journey to mastering the mind is lifelong, but every step brings you closer to unlocking the greatest power you possess: your mind. By implementing the strategies in this book—understanding motivation, controlling thoughts, thinking positively, leading yourself and others, and harnessing the power of your subconscious—you will not only change your life but also inspire those around you.